This book is a gift of the
Cops 'n' Kids Literacy Program

To: _____

From: _____

Date: _____

QUOTA *International of Bethlehem*   DeSales University

THE
IROQUOIS
INDIANS

THE JUNIOR LIBRARY OF
AMERICAN INDIANS

THE
IROQUOIS
INDIANS

Victoria Sherrow

CHELSEA HOUSE PUBLISHERS
New York   Philadelphia

7191

FRONTISPIECE: This portrait of Mohawk chief Hendrick was painted in 1710 when he was visiting Queen Anne in London. He is shown holding a wampum belt as a sign of peace and standing beside a wolf, a symbol of his clan.

CHAPTER TITLE ORNAMENT: Two figures from the Washington Covenant belt. The longest wampum belt in existance today, it was made in the late 1700s to commemorate a peace agreement between the Iroquois tribes and the 13 American colonies.

Chelsea House Publishers
EDITOR-IN-CHIEF   Richard S. Papale
MANAGING EDITOR   Karyn Gullen Browne
COPY CHIEF   Philip Koslow
PICTURE EDITOR   Adrian G. Allen
ART DIRECTOR   Maria Epes
ASSISTANT ART DIRECTOR   Howard Brotman
MANUFACTURING MANAGER   Gerald Levine
SYSTEMS MANAGER   Lindsey Ottman
PRODUCTION COORDINATOR   Marie Claire Cebrián

The Junior Library of American Indians
SENIOR EDITOR   Liz Sonneborn

Staff for THE IROQUOIS INDIANS
COPY EDITOR   David Carter
EDITORIAL ASSISTANT   Michele Berezansky
DESIGNER   Debora Smith
PICTURE RESEARCHER   Lisa Kirchner
COVER ILLUSTRATOR   Vilma Ortiz

3 5 7 9 8 6 4

Library of Congress Cataloging-in-Publication Data

Sherrow, Victoria.
   The Iroquois Indians/by Victoria Sherrow.
      p.   cm.
   Includes index.
   Summary: Examines the history, culture, and future prospects of the Iroquois people.
   ISBN 0-7910-1655-2
   1. Iroquois Indians—Juvenile literature. [1. Iroquois Indians.
2. Indians of North America.] I. Title. II. Series.
E99.I7S52   1992   92-7357
973'.04975—dc20   CIP
                                                        AC

CONTENTS

CHAPTER 1
The Sky People
7

CHAPTER 2
The Struggle for Peace
13

CHAPTER 3
Years of Peace and Plenty
23

CHAPTER 4
Changes from the Outside
35

PICTURE ESSAY
Faces of the Spirits
41

CHAPTER 5
A Shrinking World
55

CHAPTER 6
Blending Old Ways and New
67

Chronology
76

Glossary
77

Index
78

According to the Iroquois' ancient stories, the Good Twin made the earth safe for humans by defeating his brother, the Evil Twin, in battle.

CHAPTER 1

The Sky People

Long ago, before there were human beings, before the earth and the sun existed, the Sky People lived high in the heavens. Their ruler was the great Sky Chief. In the Sky World, light glowed from the large white flowers of a heavenly tree that grew in front of the Sky Chief's lodge.

The Sky Chief married a beautiful young wife. The Sky People rejoiced when they heard that Sky Woman would soon give birth to a child. But one mean-spirited being called Firedragon set out to cause trouble. Firedragon told the Sky Chief that the child his wife carried was not his.

The Sky Chief was filled with jealousy. In his anger, he jerked the light-giving tree out by its roots. Then he pushed his wife through the giant hole that was left in the ground.

Sky Woman plunged out of the Sky World. She would have fallen into the deep seas below, but some birds flew beneath her. They carried her on their backs and drifted gently down toward the water. Water animals saw Sky Woman coming, so they hurried to prepare things. Muskrat dove into the water and rose up with a large mouthful of dirt. He put this on Turtle's back and created the world for Sky Woman to land on.

A great light began to shine from above. The white flowers of the heavenly tree gleamed through the hole in the ground where the tree had fallen. This light became the sun. As sunlight touched the earth, trees and grass began to grow.

The birds set Sky Woman down on the newly made world. Soon she gave birth to a daughter. The daughter grew up and had twin boys of her own. The firstborn became known as the Good Twin. The other boy was evil from the start of his life. He even refused to wait his turn to be born. Instead he pushed his body out through his mother's side, and she died.

Sky Woman sadly buried her daughter. On the grave, wonderful plants sprang up—corn, tobacco, beans, and squash—providing the things that would later be useful to human beings.

As they grew up, the Good Twin and the Evil Twin became enemies. The Good Twin went about the earth making useful things, such as rivers, streams, plants, and animals. The Evil Twin followed his brother and caused harm wherever he went. He put rapids and rocks in the rivers and streams. He made poisonous plants, fierce animals, and terrible diseases.

The twins battled each other mightily, but in the end the Good Twin won out. He created human beings to enjoy all the wonders he had placed on earth.

The tale of the Sky People is a creation story—one that tells how the earth and human beings came to be. This story has been told for hundreds of years by North American Indians who call themselves Houdenosaunee (hoo-dee-noh-SHAW-nee), or People of the Longhouse. Early French explorers in North America gave them the name Iroquois.

At one time the Iroquois lived along the lakes and rivers in what is now upper and central New York State. After years of war,

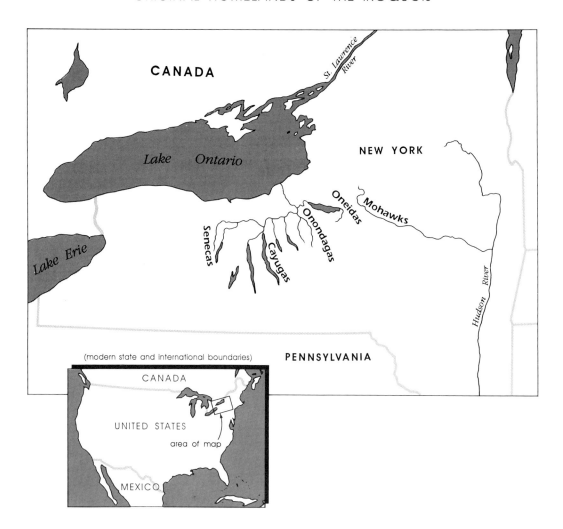

five tribes—the Mohawks, Oneidas, Onondagas, Cayugas, and Senecas—formed a powerful nation known as the *Iroquois Confederacy*. Centuries later, another tribe, the Tuscaroras, joined the group.

Well-organized villages with council meetings and elected leaders gave the Iroquois a stable way of life. Hunting and farming provided a steady supply of food.

During the 1600s, Europeans came to Iroquois territory. Sometimes the Iroquois made peace with them; at other times they fought. After the American Revolution (1776–81), the new United States government wanted the Iroquois lands free for European settlement. The government moved the Iroquois onto reservations in New York and Canada.

Today Iroquois live in many places, both on and off reservations. They work in a variety of trades, businesses, and professions. Some still follow the traditional ways, maintaining the languages and ceremonies of earlier days. As in the past, they still gather around winter campfires to hear the tale of the Sky People and other stories about Iroquois life. ▲

Hiawatha grieving for the death of his three daughters. In his hand, he holds a string of shell beads called wampum.

CHAPTER **2**

The Struggle for Peace

 The sun must love war." These words were spoken hundreds of years ago by members of the tribes that later joined together to form the Iroquois Nation. In those days, people lived in constant fear of the fighting between different tribal groups. No one felt safe from attack. That is why they said that the sun was always shining upon a war.

Originally, the Iroquois groups lived in separate territories. The Mohawks lived to the east, along what is now called the Mohawk River. West of them were the Oneidas. Farther west lived the Onondagas, the Cayugas, and the Senecas.

Villages were built in cleared areas of the forests, near a source of water and enough good soil for growing crops. The people built strong wooden stockades around their villages to protect themselves from attack.

The Indians fought for various reasons. Sometimes, one group wanted to use hunting grounds and fishing areas ruled by other people. At other times, they fought for revenge. According to their code of honor, if one group attacked another, that group was supposed to attack in return. If a member of one group killed someone from another group, he was marked for death by his victim's tribe. Warriors were called cowards if they did not strike back.

The Mohawks were among the fiercest warriors. They called themselves the Gani-engehaka (People of the Flint Country), but their enemies called them Mowaks, or "man-eaters." That is how they got the commonly used name, Mohawks. Other Iroquois feared the Mohawks. So did the Mahicans, the Abenakis, and other tribes that lived near them.

In addition to the danger from outside enemies, villagers were often afraid of their own tribe members. Anyone who spoke about peace between the tribes ran the risk

Thadodaho, an Onondaga chief, had hair so twisted that he looked as though snakes were crawling around his head. The Iroquois believed his appearance was proof of his evil nature.

of being laughed at, punished, or even killed. Some warriors terrified whole villages with their threats and demands. The most feared of these men was an Onondaga chieftain named Thadodaho. People who disagreed with him had been known to die or to disappear from the village. This led people to think that Thadodaho had magical powers and could cause people to get sick or die by wishing bad things upon them.

As the years passed and the violence continued, it seemed that the fear and sadness would never end. But a few brave people tried to bring peace to Iroquois country. One of them was an Onondaga chief named Hiawatha. Determined to end the wars in spite of Thadodaho, Hiawatha sent swift messengers to other villages with an important summons: Come to a grand council to talk about peace.

Tribal leaders agreed to attend the grand council. A large crowd gathered around the council fire, as was the custom. Hiawatha began to speak. Soon, Thadodaho interrupted the meeting. He and his warriors stood scattered among the crowd, looking threatening. Thadodaho's twisted hair looked like fierce snakes crawling around his head. People were afraid to speak up, so the council ended. No problems were settled.

After the council, Hiawatha's eldest daughter took sick and died. After the mourning period, Hiawatha again looked for a way to bring peace. He decided to call a second council. But Thadodaho came too. He frightened the leaders out of coming to an agreement.

Hiawatha was not ready to give up, even when his second daughter became ill and died, just as the first one had. People began to say that Thadodaho had used evil magic to kill Hiawatha's daughters. The struggle between the two men looked like a struggle between good and evil, and evil appeared to be winning.

After his second time of mourning ended, Hiawatha bravely called for a third council. Now he had only one child left, his youngest daughter. He loved her dearly and took her with him to the meeting. At the meeting, she joined other women who were gathering firewood for cooking.

As the council was about to begin, a large eagle appeared in the sky. Thadodaho saw the bird circling and told one of his warriors to kill it. Pierced by the warrior's arrow, the eagle fell to the ground not far from the place where Hiawatha's daughter was gathering wood. A group of men rushed forward to collect the eagle's prized feathers. In their hurry, they knocked over Hiawatha's daughter, trampling her to death and killing the unborn child she had been carrying.

People gathered in shock and sorrow around the dead girl. This time, Hiawatha could not be comforted. He had lost his whole family and was filled with grief. Hiawatha left his village and began to wander in the forest. His anger and sorrow were so strong that he began to think he was losing his mind. Hiawatha feared that all goodness was leaving him. Perhaps the evil of Tha-dodaho was taking over his mind.

As Hiawatha traveled east, he passed several lakes and gathered the small white shells he found near the water. He strung the shells into necklaces and hung them around his neck. He was entering the land of the Mohawks, and he wanted to wear the shells as a sign of peace.

Strings of wampum are still used in Iroquois ceremonies held to comfort people after the death of a loved one.

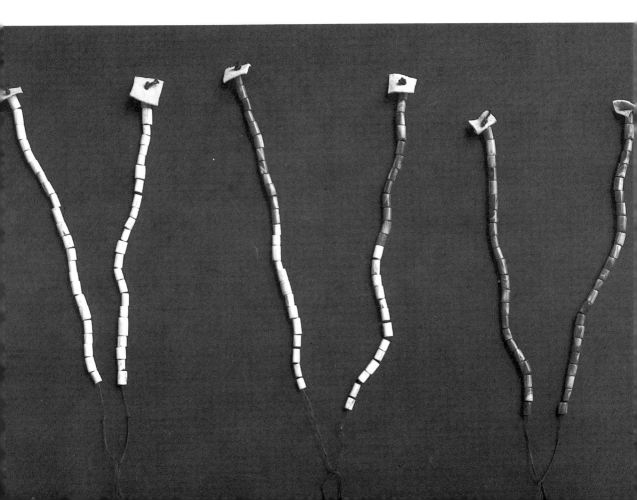

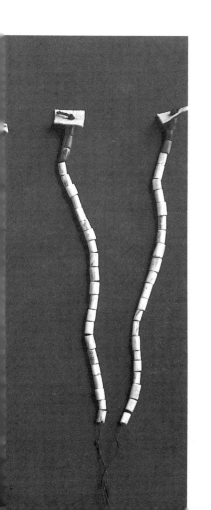

A young Mohawk woman spotted Hiawatha as he sat silently on the trunk of a fallen tree. She went back to her village and told the others about the stranger with the strings of white shells covering his chest. The village leaders sent a messenger to greet Hiawatha.

Luckily, Hiawatha had come to a place where his long search for peace would be understood. Living in this Mohawk village was Deganawida, also known as the Peacemaker. The Peacemaker had been born north of Lake Ontario, into a tribe called the Wendats (later referred to as the Hurons). From the time he was a boy, the Peacemaker said he would never become a warrior. Instead, he talked of peace and friendship among all Indians. He told his people they should stop going to war. The Peacemaker claimed that this message— the Good News of Peace—came from the Master of Life himself.

The Wendats scorned the Peacemaker's ideas, so he decided to leave his home. He paddled his canoe down Lake Ontario until he reached the Mohawk village. Because the Peacemaker was no longer a member of a hostile tribe, the Mohawks could accept his message without being called weak or cowardly. Under his influence, the villagers began to live in peace.

The Peacemaker listened as Hiawatha told of his past life and the loss of his daughters. When Hiawatha finished his tale, the Peacemaker said, "When a person has suffered a great loss caused by death and is grieving, the tears blind his eyes so that he cannot see. With these words, I wipe away the tears from your eyes so that now you may see clearly." Next, he declared that Hiawatha's ears and throat, which had been blocked by his sorrow, were now clear—he could hear, speak, and breathe freely again. Today, the Iroquois still use these words to comfort people who are mourning the loss of a loved one.

After this ceremony, Hiawatha felt stronger, and he soon became a chief among the Mohawks. Hiawatha and the Peacemaker then joined forces in a great effort—to share the Good News of Peace and bring friendship to all Indians.

Peace and unity among the Iroquois did not come quickly. Hiawatha and the Peacemaker spent the next few years meeting with tribal leaders and planning a way of government that the different people could agree on. Their plan, known as the *Great*

Peace, called for a confederacy, or partnership, of tribes.

The Mohawks were the first to accept the Great Peace and begin the new confederacy. The Oneidas thought about the plan for a year and then made a treaty with the Mohawks. With this agreement between the former enemies, the Confederacy truly began.

The Onondaga people also wanted to join the League, but their warlike chief, Thadodaho, refused to allow it. Hiawatha and the Peacemaker realized that the League could not succeed unless the Onondagas joined. Together they came up with a clever new plan to win over Thadodaho. Once again, with high hopes, they set out for Onondaga country. ▲

Corn Spirit, a sculpture carved from a moose antler by Mohawk artist Stan Hill.

CHAPTER 3

Years of Peace and Plenty

With his friend the Peacemaker, Hiawatha arrived in Onondaga country, the land of his birth. The two men knew that the Great Peace might fail if this tribe did not join them. With powerful words, they convinced Thadodaho to let them perform a special medicine ceremony—the first step in their plan.

Hiawatha and the Peacemaker sang religious songs and rubbed Thadodaho's body with herbs that were used for healing. They promised Thadodaho that he could be the League's leading chief and the fire keeper of the Confederate Council. After the ceremony, Thadodaho spoke. He said that he had changed his mind and now wished to join the League. Now that the Onondagas had joined, the Senecas soon followed.

In founding the League, the Iroquois leaders gave their people a chance to survive and prosper. The Iroquois could now raise their families in peace, doing the tasks that were necessary to stay alive. Because members of the League shared their hunting lands, the men could hunt and fish without worrying about being attacked.

Iroquois women could move about unafraid to do their job as food providers. They gathered wild nuts and berries in the forest and raised crops. Three field-grown plants were the main food of the Iroquois—corn, squash, and beans. These crops were so important that the Iroquois called them Our Supporters or the *Three Sisters*.

Iroquois women tended their crops carefully to get a good harvest. First, they planted rows of corn in small hills about three feet apart. After the cornstalks came up, the women planted bean and squash seeds in the same hills. As the bean and squash plants grew, they twined themselves around the cornstalks and rose upward instead of snaking along the ground. This made it easier to remove unwanted weeds and harvest the crops. In addition to the corn, squash, and beans, the Iroquois also grew pumpkins and some tobacco.

Some of the harvested vegetables, along with berries, meat, and fish, were dried for winter use. Getting enough food during the harsh winters was an ongoing problem. Grain was often stored in woven baskets, which the Indians buried in the ground.

Besides providing food, women played a central role in Iroquois society. The main unit of the Iroquois community was a group of relatives called an *ohwachira*. The people who made up an ohwachira traced their roots back to one woman. The eldest woman in an ohwachira was usually the head of the group.

Two or more ohwachiras made up a clan. Clan members thought of one another as family, and people took on the clan membership of their mother. Each clan had an animal name and symbol. The Mohawks and Oneidas had three clans: Turtle, Bear, and Wolf. The other tribes had these three clans and more, including Beaver, Deer, and Hawk. The head women in the ohwachiras had the honor and duty of choosing the clan leaders.

The traditional Iroquois dwelling was a bark-covered structure known as a *long-*

house. Each longhouse was shared by several related families, who placed their clan symbol over the doorway. The rooms along the sides of the longhouses served as living space; the central areas were used as meeting places for leaders and larger groups. Each town was made up of several longhouses.

Clans chose a certain number of chiefs to rule them and to work with other clan leaders to govern the village and tribe. Religion formed the common bond between clans and communities. The laws of the Iroquois directed the people to maintain the right relationship with their Creator and with other supernatural beings. Ceremonies were held to ask the spirits for help and to keep evil away.

The Iroquois lived in bark-covered dwellings called longhouses. *Each longhouse provided shelter for several families.*

Harvest times were marked with special thanksgiving ceremonies. The Green Corn Festival was held when the Three Sisters ripened in the autumn. Services were also held in the late winter or early spring, when the sap began to flow in the sugar maple trees. The Iroquois would then bore a hole in the trunk of each tree, collect the sweet sap, and boil it until it thickened into a tasty syrup. Other ceremonies of thanks were held when berries ripened or when other crops were gathered during the year.

The great New Year's or Midwinter Festival was held to give thanks after the fall hunt. People visited their neighbors with paddles, which they used to stir the ashes in their fire pits. Tribal faith keepers visited each home to announce the start of the festival, and these holy men gave thanks to the Creator for keeping the people safe all year.

A special custom in the New Year's Festival was called dream guessing. The Iroquois religion taught that dreams were important messages from supernatural beings. People were expected to follow the advice they received in their dreams. If they had a powerful dream, they told their neighbors some parts of it, then asked them to guess the rest and make the dream come true.

Sometimes the dream tellers sang and danced; at other times, they related their dreams with silent gestures. For example, a woman would show what she had dreamed by laying a digging hoe on the ground. Her neighbors might guess that she wanted a plot for planting corn. If they had guessed correctly, the tribe would then give her the land she desired.

The custom of dream guessing showed that the Iroquois understood how important the mind can be to a person's health. Dream guessing allowed people to get rid of certain worries or anger they might feel toward other tribe members. It thus helped villagers to keep the peace among themselves. When someone dreamed of hurting a person he disliked, the tribe would think of a way to fulfill the dream in a nonviolent way, such as by hitting a doll made to look like the other person.

An Iroquois ceremony known as the Traveling Rite, drawn by Jesse Cornplanter. A Seneca, Cornplanter made a series of pictures in the early 1900s that depicted Iroquois customs.

Winter was the time to gather around the fire and enjoy stories. Skilled storytellers entertained their listeners with folktales of the Iroquois people and accounts of tribal history. Stories about ghosts and supernatural creatures were always popular. Characters such as Naked Bear, Monster Mosquito, and the Great Horned Serpent clashed with witches and talking animals in these colorful stories.

Some of these supernatural beings were part of Iroquois healing customs too. The Iroquois believed that illness could result from natural causes or evil magic. They treated many diseases and injuries with herbs, plants, or cleansing rituals.

Special healers called conjurers were asked to cure people who were thought to be suffering from witchcraft or evil spells. These healers repeated special words and sang songs in order to take away the evil magic. Healers in a village sometimes joined groups called a medicine society. Society members often wore masks to show that they were experienced and respected hcalers.

The most important ceremony in Iroquois life began after the Great Peace united the tribes into the Five Nations. This great event in history is remembered each time a

A portion of the Hiawatha Wampum Belt. The pine tree in the middle represents the Iroquois Confederacy. Each square symbolizes one of the Iroquois tribes.

chief dies. A special Condolence Committee talks about the dead chief and other Iroquois leaders of the past. The ceremony comforts the mourners and welcomes the new chief, chosen by the head woman of a clan. At the ceremony, the antlers of a deer are placed on the new chief's head. Iroquois tradition says that deer antlers were chosen because deer meat feeds people and keeps them alive. The Peacemaker had said that

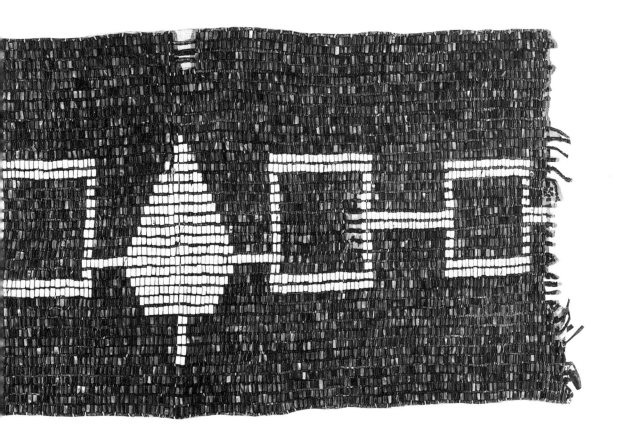

like the meat of the deer, "the Great Peace shall be the means of protecting our children hereafter."

Like the story of the Great Peace itself, these words were passed on to each new generation. Iroquois history was spoken because the people did not use written language. They also used beads made of shells as reminders of their history. These beads, which Europeans called *wampum*, were sometimes strung into belts in fancy designs with pine trees and other symbols of the Iroquois' past. Some wampum belts, including the Wing wampum belt, were displayed at meetings whenever people recited the Iroquois code of laws or discussed treaties. Wampum was also used in trade, as a form of money.

The Iroquois worked to develop their peaceful and secure way of life for centuries after the Great Peace. Fighting still took place between the Iroquois and the tribes that lived nearby. However, these wars were fought for a clear purpose—to gain land, take prisoners who could be ransomed, or get revenge—with as little killing as possible. They also gave Iroquois men a chance to prove their strength and bravery.

Warfare was to grow more violent as Europeans came to North America and began to compete for territory. The Indians soon found themselves siding with one group of Europeans or another. The newcomers had goods that were useful to the Indians. They used weapons that killed people more easily than bows and arrows. At the same time, white settlement would bring many difficult changes to Iroquois life. ▲

CHAPTER **4**

Changes from the Outside

In 1534, a French sea captain named Jacques Cartier reached the coast of North America. He sailed his ship up the great waterway now known as the St. Lawrence River, looking for a sea route to Asia. When he returned to France in 1535, he reported that he had discovered the passage to the wealth of the East.

Cartier and other explorers did not know how far away Asia was: More than 3,000

French explorer
Samuel de Champlain's
drawing of his
attack on a Mohawk
village in 1615.

miles of land lay between the Atlantic Coast, where he had landed, and the Pacific Ocean. But Europeans did know that North America contained vast amounts of open land. The new continent also provided a large supply of beaver, an animal whose fur was used to make hats and other articles of clothing. Before long, a rich *fur trade* sprang up in North America.

The Indians were skilled at trapping beaver. During the 1500s, they began exchanging furs for axes and other metal tools that the French brought from Europe. At the same time, the Mohawks and some other Iroquois also raided other tribes to get the European goods that they wanted.

These raids disturbed the trade that the French had built up with the Iroquois' neighbors. In 1609, Samuel de Champlain, the governor of New France (present-day Canada), helped several tribes fight against the Mohawks. The Indians had never faced such enemies as these Frenchmen. Champlain and his troops wore metal helmets and coats and carried fire-spouting muskets. During the first battle, Champlain killed two Mohawk chiefs and wounded a third with a single blast from his musket. The Mohawks fled under a hail of fire, leaving behind 50 dead. The following year, a party of French soldiers and their Indian allies attacked a Mohawk stronghold near the St. Lawrence, killing 80 Mohawks and taking the rest as prisoners.

After these battles, the Iroquois ended their raids in the St. Lawrence Valley for many years. At the same time, the Dutch were settling to the south and east of Iroquois country, along the Hudson River. They began to trade with the Indians and persuaded the Mohawks and Mahicans to make peace so that all could profit from the fur trade. The arrangement was good for the

Beaver, sculpted by Stan Hill. In the 17th century, Europeans were eager to trade with the Iroquois for valuable beaver pelts.

Mohawks: By trading with both the French and the Dutch, they got more guns than other tribes.

Large numbers of warriors and a good supply of guns gave the Iroquois an advantage over their enemies. Also, they lived along great rivers and lakes and could travel swiftly by water, sacking villages and capturing canoes loaded with furs. By posting lookouts along the waterways, they could spot enemies coming to attack them.

Because their old-style wooden armor was useless against European guns, the Iroquois learned to change their ways of fighting. No longer did warriors group together on the battlefield and charge the enemy head-on. Instead, they learned to hide behind rocks and trees and attack by surprise.

Enemy soldiers were just one problem the Iroquois had to face. The Europeans also brought many diseases to North America. Native Americans had never had these diseases before. They had no natural protection against them and did not know how to treat or cure them. Outbreaks of measles, influenza (flu), smallpox, lung infections, and stomach disorders caused thousands of Indians to die during the 1600s.

Despite the ravages of disease, the Iroquois made headway against competing

After many years of fighting, the Iroquois drove their Indian neighbors, the Hurons, from their homeland in 1649.

tribes while keeping the peace with the Europeans. For many years they fought fierce battles with the Hurons, causing great suffering on both sides. By 1649, many of the Hurons gathered the few belongings they had left and moved to the Ontario peninsula and to another region south of Lake Erie.

With the Hurons out of the way, the Iroquois stood to enjoy great prosperity from the fur trade. However, the presence of the Europeans created problems within the Iroquois Nation. The Mohawks had the Dutch trade all to themselves, so the other four Iroquois tribes—the Senecas, the Onondagas, the Cayugas, and the Oneidas—reached a trade agreement with the French that excluded the Mohawks. This move angered the Mohawks, who had been hoping to establish relations with the French themselves. For the first time, Iroquois tribes were competing with each other to trade with Europeans.

The Iroquois also disagreed about religion. Europeans had started church missions in Iroquois country, especially among the Onondagas. There, *missionaries* taught the Iroquois about Christianity. Those Indians who followed Christian teachings stopped taking part in their former religious customs. Many Iroquois complained about the churches and the diseases the missionaries were bringing. They attacked the missions, burning buildings and killing priests and other Europeans.

In the meantime, the Dutch lost their hold on North America. In 1664, the English

continued on page 49

FACES OF THE SPIRITS

Sacred tobacco was burned as an offering to a living basswood tree before the first carving for a False Face was done into it. Only sincere and pure men could "ask the life" and carve masks that would contain the life spirit of a tree.

Masks are often used for hiding. Trick-or-treaters, thieves, and masqueraders all wear them to disguise who they are. Among the Iroquois, masks serve another purpose. They are thought to turn the wearer into another being.

The Iroquois make two types of masks. Their False Faces are carved from wood. Their Husk Faces are woven from cornhusks—the outer covering of an ear of corn. Faces are made to look like spirits described in the Iroquois' ancient stories. The Iroquois believe that when a person puts on a Face during a religious ceremony, he or she becomes the spirit the mask represents.

The spirits symbolized by Faces are kindly and helpful to humans. They bring order to the Iroquois' world and cure the ill. The spirits can also cleanse a community, giving the people living there a fresh start with their lives.

Twice a year, in the spring and the fall, people in Faces perform such cleansing rituals. As they travel from house to house, the residents offer them gifts of tobacco, which spirits are thought to enjoy. The ceremony ends with a feast. There the Faces are given cornmeal, the favorite food of spirits. Well-fed, the spirits are expected to help the Iroquois stay healthy and happy until the next ceremony is held.

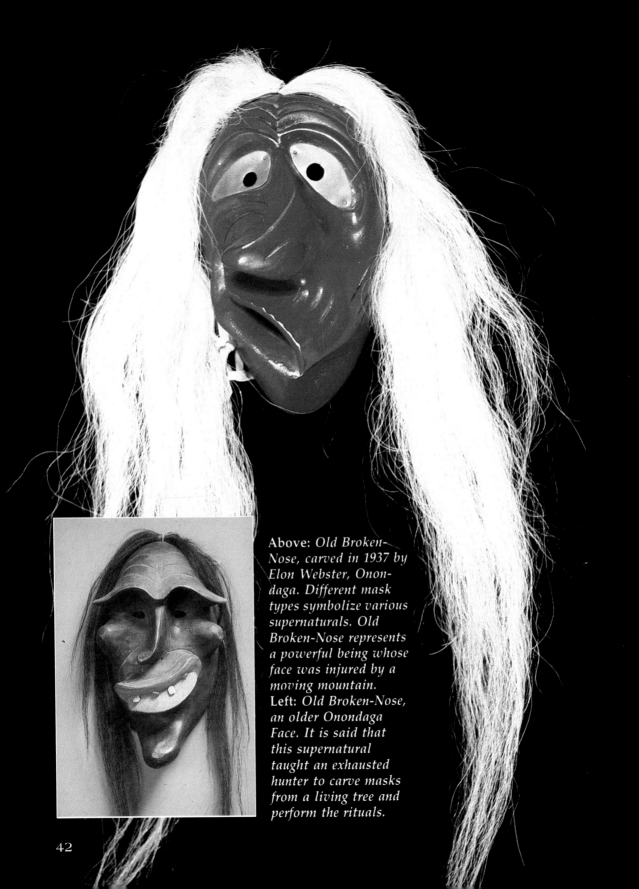

Above: *Old Broken-Nose, carved in 1937 by Elon Webster, Onondaga. Different mask types symbolize various supernaturals. Old Broken-Nose represents a powerful being whose face was injured by a moving mountain.*
Left: *Old Broken-Nose, an older Onondaga Face. It is said that this supernatural taught an exhausted hunter to carve masks from a living tree and perform the rituals.*

Above: *The Hunch-back, carved in 1943 by Robert T. Hatt, Cayuga, Six Nations Reserve, Canada. Bags of sacred tobacco attached to a mask indicate successful curing rituals.*

Right: *Seneca buffalo or devil mask, with pointed, hornlike leather ears. Iroquois masks usually have large, prominent lips, a possible reference to the practice of blowing hot ashes on an ill person during a curing ritual.*

Husk Faces, also called "bushy head" or "fuzzy hair" masks, represent the supernaturals who taught humans how to hunt and farm. They are made by women from braided dried cornhusks. **Above:** *Seneca miniature Husk Face, 4 1/4 x 4 3/4 inches, made in the 1970s.* **Left:** Fuzzy Hair Society, *watercolor by Ernest P. Smith. The artist wrote: "They are cousins of the False Face and have the same curing powers. They talk only in whispers and carry a staff to fend off all evil."*

At the Six Nations Reserve, Husk Faces are always men. On Seneca reservations in New York, women may wear masks in certain Husk Face dances, but only the men of the society perform the cures. **Above:** *Seneca Husk Face made by Mattie Young, 1970s.* **Right:** *Cayuga Husk Face made by Sayehwas, about 1932.* **Far right:** *Husk Face, Grand River Reservation.*

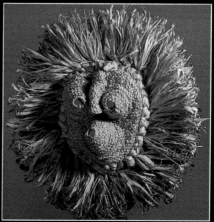

45

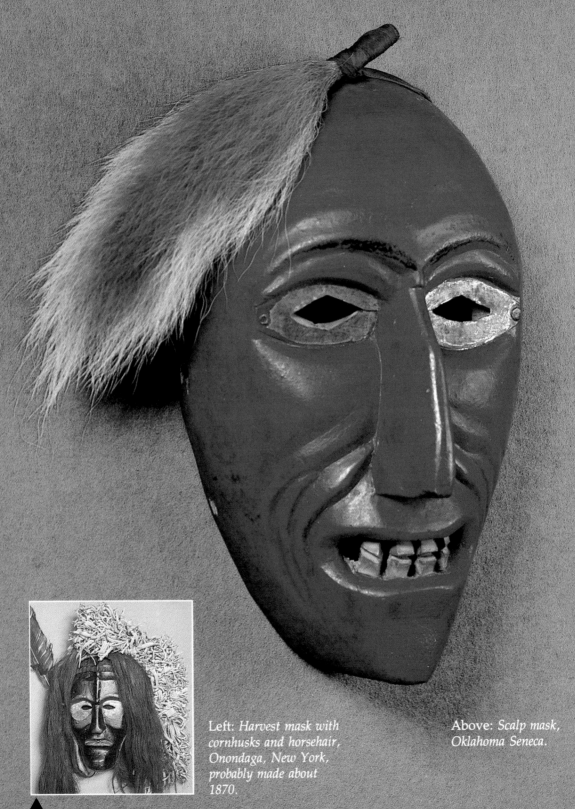

Left: *Harvest mask with cornhusks and horsehair, Onondaga, New York, probably made about 1870.*

Above: *Scalp mask, Oklahoma Seneca.*

Left: *Wolf clan mask, about 1775. Said to have belonged to Joseph Brant, this is one of the earliest Faces known.*

Above: *Whirlwind mask, Cayuga, Grand River Reservation. The extended tongue is believed to show pain. Some say that the divided face, represents a half-human, half-supernatural creature.*

Members of the False Face Society visit traditionalists'
homes during the Mid-Winter Festival. They stir ashes on
the hearths and, if the residents wish, perform curing
rituals. The Faces also conduct special ceremonies and
dances at the longhouse for the benefit of all present.
Above: *Laughing Beggar Face, Seneca, worn by boys who
visit homes and beg for tobacco at the Mid-Winter
Festival.* **Left:** *Messengers known as "Our Uncles the Big
Heads" arrive at a house. Watercolor by Jesse
Cornplanter, Seneca, about 1901.*

continued from page 40

defeated them in war and took over the territory of New Netherland, renaming it New York. The stage was now set for the 100-year struggle between France and England for control of North America. The English realized that the Iroquois, with their control of the waterways and trade routes, were valuable allies. They quickly made friends with the Iroquois and arranged for trade to go on.

On the other hand, the Iroquois' difficulties with the French continued. In 1664, the French king sent a large group of soldiers to North America to fight the Five Nations. The soldiers had clear orders from the French government to completely wipe out the enemy Indians. Hearing of this plan, the four western groups of Iroquois went to Canada and made peace with the French. The Mohawks held out until the French soldiers invaded their territory. Then they too offered to make peace.

However, the Mohawks did not really honor the peace agreement until the French soldiers burned one of their villages. The French also attacked those tribes that refused to renew the agreements. Despite the official treaties, the northern and western borders of Iroquois country remained a battleground.

While fighting with the French, the Iroquois drew closer to the English. "We are brothers and are joined by chains," the Iroquois often said of treaties they made with the Dutch and the French. Their ties with the English gave the Iroquois safe borders to the south and the east.

The wars in the west continued throughout the 17th century, and thousands of Iroquois died in battle. Homes and food supplies were destroyed. In 1700, an Onondaga leader named Teganissorens led a new peace effort. He believed that the Iroquois should be neutral—not take sides with either the French or the English. That way, the Iroquois could keep their lands and independence and avoid the crippling losses they had suffered through a century of warfare. A great speaker admired by Europeans and Indians alike, Teganissorens convinced his people to follow his ideas.

Neutrality ended the Iroquois' costly battles with the French and allowed them to trade with both sides. Individual Iroquois were free to become friendly with either group of Europeans. Some Indians joined the Catholic church as a result of their contact with the French missions. Others joined the English Protestant churches. In 1710, four Iroquois chiefs were invited to visit Lon-

Sa Ga Yeath Qua Pieth Tow was one of four Mohawk chiefs who visited the queen of England in 1710.

don, a sign that England valued their loyalty. The chiefs were treated as celebrities in London; they were wined and dined by all the leaders of English society and even called upon Queen Anne.

In the course of time, different groups of Iroquois came to prefer one side or the other in the rivalry between England and France. The Senecas and Onondagas tended to prefer the French, whereas the Mohawks were closer to the English. Nevertheless, the Iroquois as a whole maintained their neutrality during the long periods of warfare among the European powers: Queen Anne's War (1702–13), King William's War (1744–48), and the French and Indian War (1754–63). Now free from the bloodshed and destruction of war, the Iroquois rebuilt their communities and grew in strength.

The security of the Iroquois' lands attracted the Tuscaroras. This tribe from what is now North Carolina had fought brutal wars of their own against English settlers. Seeking peace, they began to move north to live with the Iroquois, to whom they were distantly related, in the 1710s. In 1722, they joined the confederacy, and the Five Nations became the Six Nations.

Unfortunately for the Iroquois, peace was short lived. In 1763, the English drove the French from Canada and became the dominant power in North America. Before long, the Iroquois became entangled in the growing conflict between England and its North American colonies. The colonists wanted to rule themselves, as a new nation. England wanted to maintain control. When the American Revolution began in 1776, fighting broke out in Iroquois territory, and the Indians were once again forced to take sides. ▲

The brilliant Mohawk leader Joseph Brant commanded both Indian and white soldiers during the American Revolution.

CHAPTER **5**

A Shrinking World

The American Revolution forced members of the Iroquois nation to make a hard choice: Should they side with the Loyalists—those colonists who wanted to keep British rule? Or should they fight alongside the Patriots, who were working toward independence? The Iroquois government allowed individual tribes and warriors to decide for themselves.

When the fighting started, the Oneidas and Tuscaroras joined the Patriots. The Mohawks, Onondagas, Cayugas, and Senecas sided with the British. In the battles that followed, Iroquois often fought against Iroquois.

Because so many of the Iroquois were siding with the British, General George Washington sent a large force into Iroquois territory in the fall of 1779. Patriot soldiers destroyed all the hostile Iroquois villages east of the Genesee River. Many Indians were left facing a harsh winter homeless and hungry. Their only choice was to take refuge in Fort Niagara, where the British provided them with food and shelter.

After suffering at the hands of the Patriots, the Loyalist Iroquois thirsted for revenge. Led by warriors such as Joseph Brant and Cornplanter, they attacked the Patriots and raided the villages of their allies, the Oneidas and Tuscaroras. The unity of the Six Nations was hopelessly shattered.

When the colonies won their freedom in 1781, the outlook was not bright for the Iroquois. They had hoped that the British would reward them for their sufferings during the war. They were shocked when the British signed a peace agreement with the Americans that gave no land rights to the Iroquois people. The Iroquois had served the British loyally. Now they were being left to the mercy of their enemies.

Eventually, one of the British generals convinced his government to provide some land for the Iroquois in Canada, which re-

A classroom of Mohawk children in 1786. The girls and boys are dressed in English clothes but wear Mohawk earrings and hairstyles.

mained under British control. Many Mohawks and other Loyalist Iroquois went north to the new territory. This area, located along the Grand River on the Ontario peninsula, became known as the Grand River Reservation. Only a small group remained in New York, and even they moved up north near the Canadian border. In order to maintain their unity, the Iroquois moved their council fire to Buffalo Creek, now the city of Buffalo, New York. For many years, the Iroquois met at Buffalo Creek to discuss important issues.

The victorious Americans, faced with the task of building the nation that became the United States, were eager to make peace with the Iroquois. The Iroquois were in a poor bargaining position; with the British gone, they had no military power. In 1784, the Iroquois signed the Treaty of Fort Stanwix. The Oneidas and Tuscaroras, who had fought alongside the Patriots, were allowed to keep their lands. The new government, however, took large portions of land from the other four tribes. The Iroquois were also told they must give up lands they held in Pennsylvania. For this property, they got only $5,000 worth of goods.

Despite their weakness, the Iroquois council of the Six Nations voted to reject the Treaty of Fort Stanwix. They offered to give back the goods they had received for their land. The Americans replied, however, that the treaty was in force, no matter what the Iroquois Confederacy said.

The Canadian Iroquois now had to adjust to life on a small tract of land called a *reservation.* The reservation included much less land than they had had before, not nearly enough to allow them to hunt and fish as they were used to doing. Leaders such as Joseph Brant helped the Iroquois find a new way of life. He showed his people how to raise herds of animals for meat instead of hunting. He also convinced men to take up farming. At first, they were hesitant because that job had always been done by women. But Brant showed them that heavy plows and other new farm tools demanded the strength of a man.

The Iroquois at Grand River also had problems with the Canadian government. The Canadians did not want the Indians to sell or rent their land. The Indians thought they had a right to use their land as they wished. Even when they did so, they often did not get the money they were entitled to. They did not understand the non-Indian ways of writing agreements to sell or rent land. Through the years, the Iroquois lost more than 350,000 acres of their land to dishonest whites.

Even the Iroquois in New York, who had been rewarded for their support of the Patriots, began to lose their lands. By 1800, they owned just a few small reservations. The government had kept insisting that the

Indians sell them land for the growing number of non-Indian settlers. The Oneida reservation shrank to only a few acres. The Cayugas gave up all their land and moved to Buffalo Creek.

In return for their land, the Iroquois got tools, farm animals, cloth, firearms, and other items they wanted. These goods made life easier, but as time passed, the people found that selling their land took away much of their independence. They

The Mohawks' Grand River settlement, as it appeared in the 1820s.

had few places to hunt, farm, or fish. Their small reservations were surrounded by non-Indian settlements. Their old power and ways of making a living were gone.

Life on the reservations was hard, especially for Iroquois men. They were no longer needed as warriors. Hunting was only allowed in a small area. White men ruled the country, and fewer Indians were needed to lead their communities. The changes did not affect women as much. They had their usual jobs as mothers, housekeepers, and farmers.

Some non-Indians were concerned about the Indians' future. A religious group called the Society of Friends—usually known as the Quakers—had settled in Pennsylvania and other colonies. In 1798, the Quakers began working with the Senecas who lived on the New York–Pennsylvania border. Unlike most whites, the Quakers did not tell the Iroquois what religion to follow. Instead, they taught the Indians reading, writing, arithmetic, and work skills that would help them make a living. The Quakers also urged the Indians to take care of their health and to retain their close-knit family life. The Seneca chief Cornplanter approved of the Quakers and helped them to work with his people.

Cornplanter's brother, Handsome Lake, became a great religious leader. At one point in his life, Handsome Lake had become so ill from drinking alcohol that he had to stay in bed. His condition worsened until it appeared that he was dead. But then he arose and told the people about a vision in which he heard a message from the Creator. The Creator wanted the Iroquois to live better lives, said Handsome Lake. They must stay away from alcohol, take better care of their families, keep up their Indian religious ceremonies, and learn useful work, such as farming.

The new religion based on these ideas, called the *Good Word*, spread from the Senecas to other Iroquois. It helped them meet the changing needs of their villages. Today, this religion is called the New Religion. Iroquois who follow traditional ways still base their religion on Handsome Lake's teachings.

Beginning in 1830, the U.S. government tried to move Indians who lived in the East to reservations west of the Mississippi River. The population of the United States was growing rapidly, and the government wanted the land for non-Indian settlers. Because of this policy, the Ohio Iroquois moved to Indian Territory, in what is now Oklahoma.

In 1838, the Senecas faced similar hardship. After the Ogden Land Company cheated them out of their land in New York, the government told the Senecas to resettle in Kansas. After years of struggle, the Senecas were able to buy back the land in 1857. After this, they were not disturbed again for nearly 100 years.

Religious leader Handsome Lake preaching to his followers in a drawing by Jesse Cornplanter.

By the late 19th century, Iroquois life had improved in some ways. Men had taken to farming, and many were successful. Others studied new trades, such as carpentry. Iroquois children, and even some adults, were attending schools both on and off the reservations. Some Iroquois went on to college.

Perhaps the best-known Iroquois during the 1800s was a Seneca named Ely S. Parker. After attending college, Parker began his career as an interpreter for the Senecas in their dealings with the U.S. government. He later studied engineering and law and joined the U.S. Army during the Civil War, rising to the rank of brigadier general. After the war, Parker became the first Indian to serve as the government's commissioner of Indian affairs.

Parker also contributed greatly to Iroquois culture through his friendship with Lewis Henry Morgan, a white lawyer. Having grown up in Upstate New York, Morgan had been interested in Iroquois history and customs for a long time before he met Parker. Parker introduced Morgan to some prominent Senecas and helped him write a number of books about the Iroquois that soon became classics.

Morgan's writings sparked wide interest in the Iroquois. Other scholars, both Indian and non-Indian, began to study the Iroquois. As a result, the Iroquois became one of the best-known of all Indian peoples. Each new generation of Iroquois was able to learn about the history and customs of their ancestors. In this way, the Iroquois have been able to preserve their rich heritage down to the present day. ▲

Two Oneida boys on a Wisconsin farm in 1901.

CHAPTER **6**

Blending Old Ways and New

The 1900s brought more changes in the Iroquois' way of life. For hundreds of years, groups of Iroquois families had lived together in their bark-covered longhouses. Families were led by elder women, who farmed the land and were thought of as the land's owners.

Changes came as men started to farm. Even though reservation land legally belonged to all Indians living on it, Iroquois men began to rent out land they were not using for farming. At the same time, the Iroquois began to live as single families in separate houses. The men now emerged as the heads of their families.

67

These changes sometimes threatened the age-old unity of the Iroquois. For example, the New York Senecas divided into two groups. Each group had its own leaders and government. One group, who became known as the Seneca Nation, decided to vote for new chiefs and write a new constitution. The other group, known as the Tonawandas, kept the more traditional style of leadership. The senior women in the group still chose chiefs to guide the people.

In Canada, the Iroquois tradition of elder women choosing the tribal leaders was ended by the government in 1924. From that time on, Canadian Iroquois have elected their chiefs. But clan mothers still name the chiefs that carry out the tribe's religious ceremonies. At the present time, only the Onondaga, Tonawanda, and Tuscarora reservations in New York State still follow the old method, which dates back to the days of Hiawatha.

In the midwestern United States, the modern Iroquois have often struggled to survive. For example, the Oneidas living in Wisconsin lost much of their land due to a law passed in 1887. At that time, the U.S. government broke up the reservations into small pieces of land. The government gave these plots to individual Indians. But the Indians had no money to pay the taxes that cities and states collect each year from property owners. The Oneidas lost almost all of their Wisconsin reservation. Their tribal government also fell apart during these hard times.

By the 1930s, the government realized that the laws governing Indian affairs were unfair. The Indian Reorganization Act, passed by the U.S. Congress in 1934, helped tribes such as the Wisconsin Oneidas to buy back some of the land they had lost. The Oneidas then wrote a new set of laws that allowed both men and women to vote and serve as tribal leaders. After that, the tribe started new businesses and built several community buildings. They also built the Oneida Museum, which holds important items from the tribe's history.

Today, the Iroquois in both Canada and the United States blend old ways with new ones. Most of them live much like their non-Indian neighbors. Few are now full-time farmers. Modern farms need large amounts of land and expensive machines to plant and harvest crops. For this reason, most farms are run by large corporations. Most Iroquois therefore work at other jobs and just grow vegetables for their own use in household gardens.

Many Iroquois make their living in factories or as construction workers. The Iroquois have a reputation as skilled ironworkers. Some have traveled all over the United States to help put up bridges and tall buildings.

Modern Iroquois women, like non-Indian women, play important roles both in and outside the home. Because there are more jobs off the reservations, many Iroquois families have moved to cities in New York and other states. The largest groups of non-reservation Iroquois live in Buffalo, Rochester, Niagara Falls, and Brooklyn, New York. Some of the Wisconsin Oneidas have settled in the city of Milwaukee.

College-educated Iroquois enter professions such as teaching, nursing, social work, law, and medicine. A number of Iroquois have served in government on the local, state, and national levels. A leading example is Robert L. Bennett, an Oneida from Wisconsin, who headed the Bureau of Indian Affairs from 1966 to 1969.

A number of Iroquois have been leaders in the fight for Indian rights. One of their greatest triumphs came in 1924, when Congress passed a law forbidding Indians to cross the border between Canada and the United States. Paul K. Diabo, a Canadian Mo-

As president of the Seneca Nation, George Heron led the fight to prevent the U.S. government from building a dam on Seneca land in the 1950s.

hawk, and Clinton Rickard, a Tuscarora from New York, led the fight against the law. They pointed out that a 1794 treaty had given Indians the right to cross the border whenever they wished. Rickard founded the Indian Defense League of America to educate non-Indians and pressure the government. After four years of struggle, the courts upheld the 1794 treaty, and Congress passed a new law enforcing the right of Indians to cross the border.

The Indian Defense League of America continued its work after winning the border dispute. Today, the Indian Defense League is the oldest organization dedicated to protecting the rights of all Indians. Members of the league support laws that will treat Native Americans fairly. They study the problems of Indians and work for better housing, education, and jobs, among other things.

Iroquois still celebrate Rickard's 1928 victory with Border Crossing Day, held each year on the third Saturday in July. Many of those taking part wear their traditional costumes. The ceremonies include a march across the border, speeches, dancing, sports, and a crafts fair.

Like other Indians, the Iroquois have had to adjust to many changes in government policies. During the 1940s and 1950s,

the Bureau of Indian Affairs decided that Indians should leave the reservations and mix
with the rest of society. For this reason, the
bureau ended many programs that had improved life on the reservations.

The Iroquois in New York fought against
these ideas. They knew that the bureau's
plan was only causing new problems for
many Indians, who were now losing even
more of their land. Those who did move to
the cities found it hard to change their way
of life and get decent jobs. More and more
Indians fell into poverty. Finally, the government realized that the new policies were
doing more harm than good and ended the
efforts to force the Indians off their reservations.

The Seneca people faced another cruel
loss in the 1950s. At that time, the U.S. Army
Corps of Engineers planned to build a dam
near Warren, Pennsylvania. This land was
on the Cornplanter Reservation, where
many Senecas lived. The Iroquois said that
taking that land would go against a treaty
the U.S. government had signed in 1794.

The Senecas fought hard to keep the
dam from being built. They wrote newspa-
per articles and talked about the problem on
television. The Seneca Nation hired an en-
gineer to study the land and design another

way to build the dam nearby. The Senecas' plan would have saved the Indian lands while still controlling floods in the area.

Despite the efforts of the Senecas, the government built the Kinzua Dam as it had planned. As a result, more than 9,000 acres of Seneca land were flooded, and 130 families had to leave their homes. The government gave the Senecas money, but they would much rather have kept their land. The Senecas who lost their homes still speak about the dam with great sadness.

A team of Mohawks playing lacrosse. Lacrosse is similar to a game played by the Iroquois for hundreds of years.

A few years later, the Tuscaroras living near Niagara Falls also fought against building on their land. The government wanted this part of Tuscarora land as a reservoir—a body of water stored for public use. When the workers came to start work on the reservoir, the Indians marched in protest. Some of them lay down in front of the trucks. Others carried signs and shouted at the workers, trying to drive them away.

In 1960, the U.S. Supreme Court ruled against the Tuscaroras, and the government built the reservoir. Still, the Tuscaroras' fight made many people understand how deeply the Iroquois cared about their land and how unfairly they were being treated. Other Indian groups were inspired by the Tuscaroras to mount protests of their own when their way of life was threatened by outsiders.

Once the Iroquois roamed over millions of acres of land. The reservations of today are much smaller, but they mean a great deal to the Iroquois. As long as they have their own land, they can maintain their history, religion, and culture. Those who have left the reservation can come home to see their relatives and take pride in their Indian heritage. In this way, the Iroquois can continue to move forward while honoring their rich traditions. ▲

CHRONOLOGY

ca. 1500	Hiawatha and the Peacemaker found the Iroquois Confederacy
1534	French explorer Jacques Cartier sails up the St. Lawrence River through Iroquois territory
1609–15	Samuel de Champlain, governor of New France, assists the Iroquois' Indian enemies in attacks against the Mohawks
1649	The Iroquois drive the Hurons from their homeland and become the most powerful Indians in the northeastern fur trade
1722	The Tuscaroras join the Iroquois Confederacy
1779	Colonial forces attack and destroy Iroquois villages during the American Revolution
1784	The Iroquois sign over much of their land to the United States in the Treaty of Fort Stanwix
1799	Seneca leader Handsome Lake founds the Good Word religion
1838	Ogden Land Company cheats the Senecas out of land at Buffalo Creek
1927	Clinton Rickard, a Tuscarora, founds the Indian Defense League of America
1950s	U.S. Army Corps of Engineers constructs dam on Cornplanter Reservation despite protests of the Senecas
1966	Oneida Robert L. Bennett named head of Bureau of Indian Affairs

GLOSSARY

fur trade	trade network in which Indians gave Europeans animal furs in exchange for metal tools and other European goods
The Good Word	a religion created in 1799 by a Seneca named Handsome Lake, who told his followers to avoid alcohol, strengthen their family ties, and take up farming; today called the New Religion
The Great Peace	Hiawatha and the Peacemaker's plan for uniting the Iroquois tribes
Iroquois Confederacy	the political union of six powerful Indian tribes (Mohawks, Senecas, Oneidas, Cayugas, Onondagas,and Tuscaroras); also called the Iroquois League, the Iroquois Nation, or the Six Nations
longhouse	a large, bark-covered dwelling that housed several Iroquois families
missionaries	Men and women who sought to teach Indians about the Christian faith
ohwachira	a group of Iroquois relatives who trace their roots back to a single woman
reservation	land set aside by the U.S. or Canadian government for use by a specific group of Indians
Three Sisters	the Iroquois' name for corn, squash, and beans, which traditionally provided them with most of their food
wampum	shell beads that were strung into belts in patterns that included symbols of events in Iroquois history; also used as money by Iroquois and European traders

INDEX

A
Abenakis, 14
American Revolution, 53, 55–56
Anne, queen of England, 52

B
Bear clan, 25
Beaver, 36
Beaver clan, 25
Bennett, Robert L., 70
Border Crossing Day, 72
Brant, Joseph, 56, 69
Brooklyn, New York, 70
Buffalo, New York, 58, 70
Buffalo Creek, New York, 58, 60
Bureau of Indian Affairs, 70, 73

C
Canada, 53, 56–59, 68, 70
Cartier, Jacques, 35
Cayugas, 10, 13, 40, 55, 60
Champlain, Samuel de, 36
Christianity, 40
Clans, 25–26
Civil War, 64
Condolence Committee, 31
Cornplanter, 56, 61
Cornplanter Reservation, 73

D
Deer clan, 25
Deganawida. (See Peacemaker)
Diabo, Paul K., 70, 72
Dream guessing, 27, 29
Dutch, the, 37, 38, 40, 51

E
Eire, Lake, 39
England, 40, 49, 51, 52, 53, 55, 56

F
Farming, 24–25, 64, 67, 69
Fort Niagara, 56
Fort Stanwix, Treaty of, 58
France, 35, 36, 38, 40, 49, 51, 53

French and Indian War, 52
Fur trade, 36–40

G
Ganiengehaka, 14
Genesee River, 56
Good Word, 62
Grand River, 57
Grand River Reservation, 57, 59
Great Horned Serpent, 30
Great Peace, 21, 23, 32
Green Corn Festival, 27

H
Handsome Lake, 62
Hawk clan, 25
Hiawatha, 16–21, 23
Houdenosaunee, 9
Hudson River, 37
Hurons, 19, 39–40

I
Indian Defense League of
    America, 72
Indian Reorganization Act, 69
Indian Territory, 63
Influenza, 38
Iroquois
    and American Revolution,
        55–56
    ceremonies, 26–32, 72
    chiefs, 26, 30–32, 68
    Confederacy, development of,
        10, 13–21, 23–24
    creation story, 7–9
    diet, 24–25
    and disease, 38
    and Europeans, 11, 36–40,
        49–53
    healing customs, 30
    housing, 25–26, 67
    and Indian rights movement,
        70–72
    preservation of history, 32,
        64–65

INDEX

religion, 26, 40, 62
reservation life, 58–61, 67, 75
societal structure, 25, 67
storytelling, 30
in twentieth century, 67–75
warfare, 32–33, 36–39, 49, 51
women's roles, 24–25, 70

K
King William's War, 52
Kinzua Dam, 74

L
London, England, 52
Longhouse, 26, 67

M
Mahicans, 14, 37
Medicine society, 30
Milwaukee, Wisconsin, 70
Missionaries, 40, 51
Mohawk River, 113
Mohawks, 10, 13, 14, 18–21, 25,
    36–37, 40, 49, 55, 57
Morgan, Lewis Henry, 64–65

N
New Year's Festival, 27
New York, 49, 57, 59, 63, 68, 73
Niagara Falls, New York, 70, 75
North Carolina, 52

O
Ogden Land Company, 63
Ohwachira, 25
Oneida Museum, 69
Oneidas, 10, 13, 21, 25, 40, 55, 56,
    58, 60, 68–69, 70
Onondagas, 10, 13, 21, 23–24, 40,
    52, 55, 68
Ontario, Canada, 57
Ontario, Lake, 19

P
Parker, Ely S., 64

Peacemaker, 19–21, 23, 31
Pennsylvania, 58, 61
Protestantism, 51

Q
Quakers, 61
Queen Anne's War, 52

R
Reservation, 59, 61, 68–69, 73
Rickard, Clinton, 72
Rochester, New York, 70
Roman Catholicism, 51

S
St. Lawrence River, 35, 37
Seneca Nation, 68, 73
Senecas, 10, 13, 24, 40, 52, 55, 61,
    63, 64, 68, 73–74
Smallpox, 38
Society of Friends See Quakers
Sugar maple trees, 27
Supreme Court, U.S., 75

T
Teganissorens, 51
Thadodaho, 15–18, 21, 23–24
Three Sisters, 24, 27
Tonawandas, 68
Turtle clan, 25
Tuscaroras, 10, 52, 55, 56, 58, 68,
    75

U
U.S. Army, 64
U.S. Army Corps of Engineers, 73

W
Wampum, 32
Warren, Pennsylvania, 73
Washington, George, 56
Wendats. See Hurons
Wing wampum belt, 32
Wisconsin, 68, 69
Wolf clan, 25

ABOUT THE AUTHOR

VICTORIA SHERROW holds B.S. and M.S. degrees from Ohio State University. The author of numerous stories and articles, she has also written 3 picture books and 16 works of nonfiction for children, including *Phillis Wheatley* in Chelsea House's JUNIOR WORLD BIOGRAPHY series. Sherrow lives in Connecticut with her husband, Peter Karoczkai, and their three children.

PICTURE CREDITS